I0011177

Kindle Fire HDX: The Beginner's User Guide

The Basic Guide to Master the HDX Tablet

Many HDX owners are not making the most of their new device; learn the ins and outs of your HDX and maximize your efficiency, entertainment, and productivity!

By

Robert Walden
Tech Specialist & User Guide Author

Table of Contents

What's Inside Your HDX Box?

Enclosed in your Kindle Fire HDX box you can expect to find:

One Kindle Fire HDX Tablet
You will receive one of the two size models (7" or 8.9")

One USB Cable
The USB Cable is for charging the Kindle Fire HDX (when connected via the power adapter). It can also be used to move files off of other devices and onto the Kindle.

One Power Adapter
This connects to your USB cable; making a charger to be used in an outlet.

A Quick Start Manual
A brief set of directions to begin enjoying the Kindle Fire HDX right away.

HDX Specifications

	Kindle Fire HD	Kindle Fire HD 8.9	Kindle Fire HDX	Kindle Fire HDX 8.9
Cost	Starts at $139	Starts at $229	Stars at $229	Stars at $379
Screen	7-inch	8.9-inch	7-inch	8.9-inch
Screen Resolution	1280x800 (216 ppi)	1920x1200 (254 ppi)	1920x1200 (323 ppi)	2560x1600 (339 ppi)
Processor	1.5 GHz Dual Core	1.5 GHz Dual Core	2.2 GHz Quad Core	2.2 GHz Quad Core
Battery	10 hours	10 hours	11 hrs / 17 hrs while reading	12 hrs / 18 hrs while reading
Audio	Dolby, Dual Stereo Speakers	Dolby, Dual Stereo Speakers, Built-in Mic	Dolby, Dual Stereo Speakers, Built-in Mic	Dolby, Dual Stereo Speakers, Built-in Mic
Wi-Fi	Dual band	Dual band & Dual antenna	Dual band & Dual antenna	Dual band & Dual antenna
4G Capability	None	Yes	Yes	Yes
Camera	No Camera	Front-facing (HD)	Front-facing (HD)	Front-facing (HD) & Rear-facing (8MP)
Hard Drive	8GB or 16GB	16GB, 32GB or 64GB (only on 4G)	16GB, 32GB or 64GB	16GB, 32GB or 64GB
Weight	12.2oz	20oz	Wi-Fi: 10.7oz, 4G: 11oz	Wi-Fi: 13.2oz, 4G: 13.5oz
Support	Email, Phone, Web	Email, Phone, Web	"MayDay" button, email, phone + web	"MayDay" button, email, phone + web
Software	Fire OS 3.0 "Mojito"	Kindle Fire OS 2.0	Fire OS 3.0 "Mojito"	Fire OS 3.0 "Mojito"

HDX 7" Specs

Kindle Fire HDX devices with 7-inch screens can store 16GB, 32GB or 64GB of data.

You can choose to enable "Special Offers" when you purchase your HDX. This allows advertisements to be displayed on your screen when it is in lock mode, and it reduces the device's purchase price. There is the option to turn this feature back off by paying the discount differential after you've begun using your HDX.

You can also choose between two different Wi-Fi settings: Wi-Fi Only or WiFi + 4G for AT&T or Verizon, depending on which carrier you use. 4G will give you roaming capabilities; your HDX's data plan must be purchased and arranged by your carrier.

The HDX 7-inch displays an ultra sharp picture across the 1900x1200 display, with 323 Pixels Per Inch (PPI) and flawless color (100% sRGB). No other tablet this size has the same processing capabilities. Its 2.2Ghz quad-core processor and 2GB RAM make for video free of choppiness and a vivid experience for gamers. Every HDX comes with the new operating system from Amazon, the Fire OS 3.0 or "Mojito," pre-installed.

The HDX 7-inch has a robust battery power source that allows for 17 hours of reading on one charge, and 11 hours of heavier usage.

HDX 8.9" Specs

The Kindle Fire HDX devices with 8.9-inch screens share similarities to the 7-inch model, including the "Special Offers" setting, the Wi-Fi or Wi-Fi with 4G internet connections, and the same three data storage size options: 16GB, 32GB or 64GB.

The 8.9-inch model has a 2560x1600 screen, 339 Pixels Per Inch (PPI) and the same flawless color (100% sRGB) on a High Definition picture. At 13.2oz it is slimmer in appearance and 34% lighter than the HD version that came before it. It's also more powerful, as it's 2 GB RAM and 2.2GHz quad-core processor give it 3x as much processing power than its predecessor. Gamers greatly benefit from the incredible Adreno 330 GPU (graphics processing unit) because it is 4x as fast.

Other features on the 8.9-inch model, not found on the 7-inch, are its 8 mega-pixel rear-facing camera with LED flash and the 1080p HD video support (both versions have a smaller front-facing camera). Also, users will be rewarded with an additional hour of battery usage on one charge: 18 when reading only, 12 for heavier use.

Layout - The HDX Exterior

Your HDX outer design looks like this:

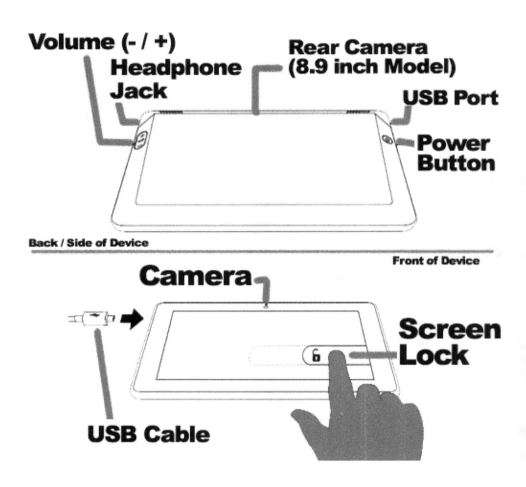

Volume (- / +)
Headphone Jack

Rear Camera (8.9 inch Model)

USB Port

Power Button

Back / Side of Device

Front of Device

Camera

Screen Lock

USB Cable

8

Back / Side of the HDX

Camera - 8 Mega Pixel, Rear-Facing – Only the 8.9inch HDX model includes the rear-facing camera feature. Equipped for 1080p HD photos and videos.

Volume – Two buttons on the back control the volume.

Headphone Input – Located adjacent to the volume buttons.

Power – Turn on/off with this button on the back.

USB Port – Located alongside the power button.

Front Side of HDX

Camera - 720 pixel HD Front-Facing – comes standard on both HDX devices.

Lock Screen – this display appears when you turn the device on (or exit sleep mode). Unlock the HDX by sliding the lock icon in the middle of the display. A password may be required if you've opted to set one up (see security settings).

Quick Starter Guide

Initial Power-Up

Press and hold the power button to start-up your HDX. The OS will boot up quickly. Slide the lock icon toward the middle of your screen and you're in!

Note: *To open programs, applications, and files on your HDX, simply tap down on the display over the icon or command in order to select it. No cursor is necessary. The same applies to operating within most applications. The other essential operational function is swiping, which is explained in a tutorial the device will run during your first use.*

A list of options for the device's primary language is available. Choose your preferred language and then hit "Continue."

You can now connect to a Wi-Fi network. A list of detected networks will appear. Enter the appropriate security credentials, if required by your network, and then select "Connect."

Next, your HDX gives you the option of incorporating social media accounts, including Facebook and Twitter. Choose "Connect Your Facebook Account" or "Connect Your Twitter Account" accordingly. You will need to enter a username and password for the corresponding accounts. Linking your HDX to these accounts will let you share content more easily to your networks. You can opt out of this option, just select "Next."

You will now arrive at the main screen. When you choose "Get Started" you will get a brief tutorial on how to utilize swiping. Understanding this is essential in order to properly use your HDX.

Using Sleep Mode

Sleep Mode puts the device in a low-power state from which it can power back up in little time.

When the device is on, press the power button and it will enter this mode.

To shut it down completely, press the power button and keep it down for at least two seconds. Follow the prompt for completion.

To power up from off, press the power button in the same manner. You will see "Kindle Fire HDX" on the screen as the Operating System boots up. This should take 30-seconds at most.

Registering Your Kindle

Your HDX may come with an Amazon account linked to it, depending on the circumstances when purchased. You need to link an account to purchase new content from Amazon or to access your media in your Amazon cloud.

HDXs that are not pre-registered must be linked manually to an Amazon account. To do this, make sure your Wi-Fi connection has been established. At the home screen, swipe down to pull up the quick settings menu. Select the settings icon, then My Account, and then "register."

To register an existing Amazon account to your HDX, simply log-in and choose Register.

If you need to create a new Amazon account, select Create Account and you will be provided with the necessary steps via Amazon's guidance.

Congratulations! Your HDX is now linked to your Amazon account and the Amazon Cloud!

Deregistering Your Kindle

Your HDX cannot be registered to multiple accounts simultaneously. In order to change accounts, you must first deregister the HDX from whichever account it is connected to. To do this on the HDX directly, swipe down to pull up the Quick Settings screen. Select Settings and then My Account. Then choose Deregister.

You can also do this on a computer by accessing your Amazon account on Amazon.com. In the "Your Account" menu to the right of the search bar, select "Manage Your Kindle." Go to the Manage Your Devices tab on the left. Once there, you will see all of the devices connected to your account. Choose the HDX device you wish to deregister and click the deregister option.

Your HDX can now be registered to another account.

Navigating Your HDX

The HDX was designed with "easy to use" navigation controls being a central focus. Larger icons and an improved main menu provide an ease of use not found in previous versions.

Rotating Your Screen

Position the HDX length-wise for "portrait orientation" or rotate it so it is positioned wider across for "landscape orientation."

This requires the Auto-Rotate option to be on. Slide down from the top of the device to pull up the Quick Settings menu. From here, you can choose to lock your device's screen orientation so it can't change, or you can unlock it so the screen will adjust to how you hold it.

Navigating the Various Screens

The Home Screen

Once the HDX has booted up and unlocked, the Home Screen will appear. Appearing on the screen (from top to bottom) you will find the Status Bar, Navigation Bar, Carousel, Home Screen Recommendations and Grid View.

The Status Bar

This narrow black bar contains basic information such as the name of the device, the time, Wi-Fi connection, and battery life.

The following indicators may be found in the status bar, with the meanings as following:

Status Bar Indicators

Your Kindle Fire is fully charged.

Your Kindle Fire needs to be charged.

Your Kindle Fire is charging.

Bluetooth is on and paired with a compatible Bluetooth device.

Bluetooth is on, but not in range or paired with a compatible Bluetooth device.

A new notification has arrived.
The number of unread notifications will appear in the circle.

Quiet Time is on.

An app or a website is using Wi-Fi to estimate your device location

Parental controls are on.

Airplane Mode is on.

Your Kindle Fire is currently mirroring its screen.

Your Kindle Fire is connected to a Wi-Fi network (strong signal).

Your Kindle Fire is connected to a Wi-Fi network (weak signa).

Your Kindle Fire is connected to a Wi-Fi network,
but can't connect to the Internet.

Navigation Bar

The Navigation Bar runs along the top of the display, just below the Status Bar. From here you can bring up any of the following features: Search, Shop, Games, Apps, Books, Music, Videos, Newsstand, Audiobooks, Web, Photos, Docs, and Offers. A short description of these is below (more in-depth descriptions can be found further along in this guide).

Search

Tap the Search Icon to engage the Search Screen. The electronic keyboard will pop up on your display. Use this to enter your search query. You can refine your search criteria to just Libraries (content stored on your HDX), Stores (the Amazon Marketplace) or Web, which will open the search to Internet results.

Note that as you begin entering your search terms on the keyboard, the device will present you with popular search options that match. You can click on these to expedite your search.

Carousel

The Carousel can be found in the middle of your screen. The files and applications you use the most will appear here. Use the swiping motion to rotate through and find the content you want to open.

To take something off the Carousel, simply press down on the icon and hold. The option "Remove From Carousel" will appear.

Home Screen Recommendations

Certain media recommendations may appear on your home screen as suggested by Amazon. You may choose to leave this or remove them.

Remove Recommendations

To take a specific recommendation off the Home Screen, simply tap down on it and hold. Then select the "Not Interested" option.

To disable recommendations as a Home Screen feature entirely, swipe down from the top of the display and locate the Settings icon from within the Quick Settings menu. From there, select Applications. Select Home Screen. From there, you can switch between Show/Hide to keep recommendations off the Home Screen.

Grid View

The Home Screen Grid View is located at the bottom of your display. Like the Carousel, it contains many of your commonly used items. In Grid View, however, they are all laid out in the traditional electronic desktop display fashion.

Tap and hold down an item's icon and then press "Remove" to take it off of your Grid View.

Conversely, as you are navigating your device you may encounter items you would like to add to Grid View. Tap and hold down any one of these items, and then select "Add to Home."

Additional Screens

Quick Settings Screen & Notification Menu

This screen will not automatically appear on your Home Screen. You must swipe downward, beginning at the uppermost part of the screen to make it appear.

It will appear as a toolbar (see below) with the HDX settings most commonly accessed.

| Auto-Rotate | Brightness | Wireless | Quiet Time | Mayday | Settings |

Press down on the icon for the setting you wish to modify and your options will be displayed.

A description of your options for each of these is below. Note that the icon labeled "Settings" will give you access to the rest of the HDX settings not found in this menu and we cover these settings in a completely separate chapter coming up.

The Auto-Rotate Setting

The Auto-Rotate setting can enable or un-enable the rotation of your display between portrait and landscape as you pivot the positioning of your HDX. When the display/positioning is set the way you would like, press the Auto-Rotate button to lock this screen's positioning. Repeat the process at any time going forward to unlock the screen, allowing it to change orientation when the tablet is moved.

The Brightness Setting

To the right of the Auto-Rotate icon is the Brightness setting. Tap the icon and then rotate the Brightness tab to set your preference.

Auto-Brightness is available to select as well. This convenient setting, when selected, changes brightness settings automatically for you based on your surroundings. It can even isolate select areas of the display that are too dark or too bright compared to the rest, and modify just them for a balanced viewing experience.

The Wireless Setting

The setting to the right of Brightness controls your Wi-Fi. It can be used to manage the following:

Airplane Mode

Airplane Mode is a quick way to shut off your wireless connectivity without having to disconnect/reconnect to a network. Some commercial flights may require you to do so to prevent interference with airplane control equipment. When this setting is on, you will see a small airplane in the upper-right corner of the screen.

Wi-Fi
Press this button to enable/un-enable wireless connectivity. If enabled, a list of detected networks will appear. Tap the network you would like to connect to and supply the security information if necessary. As with any device, avoid unsecure networks as they can expose you to a host of external threats.

Bluetooth
Bluetooth is a feature that links multiple electronic devices wirelessly. Toggle the Bluetooth button to enable/un-enable it. Once enabled, you will see an icon that looks like an antenna in the upper-right area of your Status Bar.

Next, select "Pair a Bluetooth Device" to see which devices your HDX can connect with. Typical options are: keyboards, controllers, A2DP compatible headsets, speakers, and headphones.

Note: this device does not support NFC (near-field communications), a Bluetooth feature that enables data transfer between mobile devices in proximity to each other.

Location-Based Services
When you enable this you will see an alert that says, "By enabling this feature, location data about your Kindle is sent to

Amazon and third-party apps and websites…" Tap "Continue" to allow this.

Doing so will make your physical location available to external web-based tools that can streamline your searches based on localized options, saving you the time of refining them yourself. To turn off this this feature, simply press the button once more.

The Quiet Time Setting

When on, this feature will prevent any notifications from interrupting you. You can tell your device is on "Quiet Time" if there is an icon in your Status Bar that looks like a zero with a dash crossing it. Press the Quiet Time button once more to turn the feature back off.

The Mayday Setting

This amazing new feature is designed as a helpful reference point to assist HDX users with live Amazon support. Press Mayday and you will be sent to the Amazon Assist page where you can connect with a live support person. More information about this service is provided further along in this document.

The Settings Icon

As mentioned previously, the icon labeled "Settings" gives you access to the rest of the HDX settings not found in this menu.

Notification Tray

All of your existing notifications are visible below the Quick Settings.

These notifications let you know what behind-the-scenes activities your HDX is performing while you are running an application or browsing media content.

For instance, if an email message comes in while you are watching a video, you may receive a notification if your settings allow for it. If you tap this notification, you will see options for ignoring or responding to the notification (in the email example, you would be directed to your inbox).

Swipe the notification aside to clear it, or press Clear All to remove them all.

Note: As mentioned earlier, the Quiet Time feature will prevent notifications from popping-up.

Options Bar

The options bar can be found at the bottom of your HDX (except the Home Screen).

Looking across the Options Bar from left to right:

In left corner of your screen you will see an icon that looks like a house called the Home Button. Tap the icon and you will go the Home Screen.

To the right of the House Button you will see an arrow icon pointing to the left called the Back Button. Tap the icon to back to the last screen.

To the right of the Back Button you will see an icon that looks like a list on a sheet of paper called the Menu Button. Tap the icon to pull up a menu that will allow you to provide additional settings for the screen you are on.

To the right of the Menu Button you will see an icon that looks like a magnifying glass called the Search Button. Tap the icon to view a search bar. A keyboard will also come up to allow you to type in your search terms.

If you are on a page where no Options Bar appears, tapping at a blank area of your screen should trigger an Options Bar to appear.

Navigation Panel

There is a tab for extra navigation options. These options are available for certain applications, utilities, and content libraries. From the left of the HDX, swipe across the display to the right and the Navigation Panel will appear (reverse the motion to make it disappear).

Unique Screens & Helpful Maneuvers

When Using an Application

While using an application or an eBook, tap into an open area on the display and the Options Bar will appear. You may also be presented with options tailored to the application you are in.

The Quick Switch Feature

The Quick Switch bar allows you to jump back to media you had been viewing previously. With the Options Bar up, tap and hold on the bar and then slide it toward the top of the screen. Apps, Books and Utilities that were viewed previously can be selected to view again.

The Swype to Type Feature

The keyboard comes equipped with the Swype feature, which enables you to input words at a much quicker rate. Tap on the first letter in the word you want to type. Without lifting your finger, slide it to the next letter in the word until you have hit them all.

Take your finger off the screen and confirm that the correct wording is displayed. Swype also automatically puts spaces between words, so you can move right on to the next one!

Exploring the Amazon Store & Your Content Libraries

Browsing the Amazon Store

A fundamental benefit of this device is the integration with the Amazon marketplace. Millions of books, movies, TV shows and physical products are available to you right, literally right at your fingertips.

Open the Amazon Store by tapping "Shop" on the left of the Navigation Bar. You can choose between Shop Amazon (physical product offerings), Books, Videos, Music, Games, Newsstand, Apps, Audiobooks and Amazon Prime (digital product offerings). You can also peruse the most popular Amazon Store items on a carousel at the bottom of the display.

Browsing Kindle Books

Once in the Amazon Store, select "Books" on the left hand side, to view the Book marketplace. If you have registered your device, it will already be synced with your Amazon account and will give you relevant suggestions. Here, you will see three rows of the suggestions. The top row is an alternating row of Best Sellers, Kindle Daily Deals, and other suggestions based on your browsing preferences and purchases.

The next is a row of "Recommended for You" books, which you can browse by swiping left or right. The bottom row is the "Kindle Select 25", which lists 25 exciting books for the week, curated by Amazon.

View additional items such as "Monthly Deals", "New & Noteworthy", and "Kindle Serials" by swiping up. Use the Search tool to find specific books.

After making your selection, you will arrive at a page that provides additional information about the book such as a synopsis of the content, a larger view of its cover, and the purchasing information.

Further down the page you can view other books popular with Amazon users who purchased the one you are checking out. There are also "Editorial Reviews" and "Customer Reviews" to help you learn more. Below this, you can view product information like the number of pages, when it was published, etc. There may also be an "About the Author" section.

Buying Your Kindle Books

With the book information open, choose the 'Buy for $XX.XX' option. On a registered HDX, your payment details will be on file so you will not need to re-enter them. Once it has downloaded, tap "Read Now" and enjoy your book!

Add Book Selections To A Wish List

The "Wish List" compiles Amazon books you have viewed and want to keep track of as prospective buys. To place an item on this list, tap on the book and then the "More Options" tab. A menu with the option to "Add to Wish List" will appear. After adding your selection, you will also be prompted with the option to "View Wish List" to see the all the items you have saved.

Navigating Your Content Libraries

Your Amazon account and HDX are fully integrated to be an all-encompassing catalogue for accessing any of your Amazon media.

Book Library

You can view all of your Amazon books in the Book Library by choosing "Books" from the Navigation Bar. Both, items that you have saved locally on your device, and items that are in your Amazon Cloud, can be seen.

Download Books from Cloud

Books in your Cloud can be downloaded and saved locally to your HDX.

From within the "Cloud" view, select the item you want. The transfer should take just a few seconds, after which a check mark in the lower right corner will appear. It can now be accessed directly on your HDX from wherever you are, without requiring a web connection.

Browse Books Stored On Your Device

You can restrict your view to just the books saved locally by tapping "On Device" on the top right of the screen. The "Cloud" tab to the left of it will include the items you have bought, but not yet saved on the HDX.

Music Library

Tap "Music" in the Navigation Bar to go to this library. Amazon's "Terms of Use" will come up upon your initial visit. Select "Continue" if the terms are acceptable. You can click on a link that will direct you to a page with the full listing of the terms.

Similar to your Books Library, you can choose to view items stored in the Music Library either via the "On Device" view or "Cloud" view.

No music is included with the HDX out of the box. Therefore the "On Device" tab should say, "No music on device." But if your Amazon Cloud account contains music files you can now transfer these files to your device.

Press the "Cloud" tab located to the left of the "On Device" tab. Any music purchased on your Amazon Cloud account will appear. These files can be played in the cloud if you have an active internet connection, or you can download the file from this view so they will be stored locally on your HDX to be used with a wireless connection in the future.

Playing Music

You can listen to albums in your library by using controls located at the bottom of the album's cover image.

Choosing "Play All" will play all the songs in the album. It will also initiate a menu for the playback features: Return to previous track, Pause, and Skip to next track.

There are three additional features found further to the right: Repeat play, Shuffle, and Volume control. Tap the arrow in the opposite corner of the display to return to the previous album controls.

Downloading Music To Your HDX

If you like what you hear and want to save it on your HDX, hit the "Download All" option from within the album view. When finished, the album can be found in the "On Device" section.

Once downloaded, the album's playback screen will now have the "Explore Artist" feature for learning more about the musicians you like and to find others that are comparable.

Press the Back button to return to the previous screen and the Home button to be redirected to the Home screen.

Video Library

The third library option from this toolbar is "Videos." You can find Amazon clips in this library (both film and television).

While on the "Videos" view, tap "Library" in the top right portion of the display. The layout is similar to those for Books and Music, and the "On Device" collection will also be empty when starting out. Any videos you have in the Amazon Cloud will sync-up, and they can be clicked on and downloaded to your device locally. Filter your files by "Movie" or "TV" with the menu in the upper-middle of the display.

From the top of the listing page, you will find all your current television shows arranged by season and by episode, and you can save your progress within an episode to finish at another time.

Television shows of interest can be put on your Wish List, just like books and music. Selections can be viewed in High Definition or Standard Definition, either in the Amazon Cloud or from your device if they have been downloaded.

Apps Library

Amazon has customized thousands of Android apps for use on your HDX. All of them are ready to be downloaded from the Amazon Android Marketplace to your Apps Library.

The best way to get to this library is by going into "Apps" from the main toolbar. Grid View is another way to reach it.

On the "Apps" page, all of your applications (both Cloud-based and downloaded) will be displayed. Items that have a check mark in the bottom right have already been loaded onto your device from the Amazon Cloud and can be run right away by tapping on them.

Applications that come standard with your HDX are basic like "Help", "Silk Browser", "Calendar", "Camera", "Settings", "Contacts", "Kindle Free Time" and "Shop Amazon." Additional applications that you have already added to your Amazon account will also appear.

These additional applications, and every newly added application, can be saved to your device with just a tap on the icon. They should only need a few seconds to make the transfer, taking your bandwidth and the file's storage requirements into account.

The "On Device" tab will show all the applications that have been saved on the HDX and are therefore ready for your use.

The "Cloud" tab shows the applications you have previously purchased or downloaded for free (yes there are many free apps), but not yet saved to the device. Some of these will have to be downloaded before they can be used from your HDX.

The App Content grid can be navigated either alphabetically ("By Title") or by displaying applications you have been accessing historically ("By Recent").

The Kindle (Android) App Store

Next to the "Cloud/On-Device" tabs is the "Store" feature. Tap it to enter the Kindle Android App store. Here you can browse a variety of "Featured Apps & Games" and check out suggested apps based on your buying history.

Battery

The battery on your HDX should be completely charged prior to initial usage. A power adapter and USB cable come with the device for your convenience.

Plug in the USB end of the cable into the USB port found on the side of your HDX and connect the other end of your cable into the power adapter. Then just plug the adapter into a power outlet.

Five hours is the most time required to bring the battery to 100%.

The power adapter and cable that come with your HDX are optimal for this device. Substituting different power cables/adapters may result in longer charging times.

While being charged, you will see an icon that looks like a bolt of electricity on your device in the status bar.

Battery Meter/Battery Life

The battery meter is the icon farthest to the right on your Status Bar. It is shaped like a battery, and the level at which the icon appears solid represents roughly how much of its battery life remains.

If you prefer to be shown precise readings, go to the Quick Settings menu. Select "Settings" and then "Device." From here you can turn on the "Show Battery Percentage in Status Bar."

Setting Up Wi-Fi

This guide covered setting up your home Wi-Fi in the "Initial Power Up" section.

When you take your HDX outside of this network, it will detect available wireless network in your new surroundings.

You can choose a network to connect to by going to the Quick Settings menu and then "Settings" on the top right. Choose "Wireless" and then "Wi-Fi." A "Wi-Fi Networks" menu will appear.

Network icons that have a lock next to them need passwords to be connected to. Otherwise they are open networks where no password is required.

Tap on your desired network and then "Connect." A keyboard will appear if you need to type in a password.

In Wi-Fi settings, the Wi-Fi receiver can be toggled off/on. When it is off, your device will not use up power as quickly, as you will be disconnected from the Amazon Cloud and can only access content and applications stored locally on your HDX.

How to Browse The Web

Your device comes equipped with a customized web browser called Silk. Other browsers such as Windows Explorer and Google Chrome can be used, but using Silk is your best bet to enable your device to function optimally.

Open the "Silk Browser" by tapping the icon, which is located in Grid View (the lower portion of the Home screen). The browser that pulls up will display some commonly visited sites in a grid. Over time, these will be replaced with the sites you frequent the most. Tap on the site you want to go to. If you want to exit the site, tap the "X" in the top right of the display.

The clear bar with the magnifying glass on its right side can be used to enter a web address directly or to type in search terms using the keyboard that will come up on the lower part of the display. The grid of your commonly frequented websites will also come up.

Silk's default search engine is Bing.com. Instructions for establishing a different search engine are available further along in this document under "Browsing the Internet."

Tap "Home" in the lower right of the display to exit the browser.

Advanced Settings

Settings Screen

All of your HDX's settings can be pulled up from selecting the Settings Icon from the Quick Settings menu. Let's explore each setting in-depth as these settings will control your entire user experience from security measures to entertainment options.

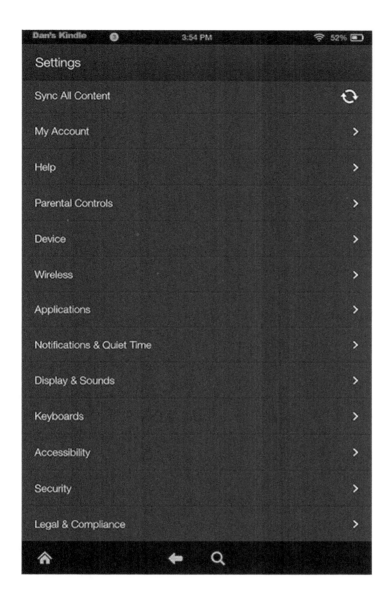

Sync All Content

This setting is located at the very top of the list. It is a fast way to link your HDX with your Amazon Cloud account to quickly give you local access on your device to all of the web-based content. Books, games, audiobooks and videos that you have purchased on Amazon and saved in the cloud can now be downloaded to your device and be enjoyed at any time (without wireless connectivity).

My Account

Under the Sync All Content setting is My Account, where the device's registration number, the device's name, your name and your Kindle email address can be found.
When you register your HDX, a Kindle Email address gets assigned. The format is typically: name@kindle.com or contact_4855@kindle.com.

Deregister

Selecting the Deregister button will generate another window that provides the option of deregistering your device. This will sever your HDX's association with your Amazon account (and all the media from that account you had been accessing on the HDX). This does not mean that those items are lost; another device can now be registered to the account and your media items can be again viewed and downloaded.

Account Settings

Underneath the Deregister button, you will find Account Settings. Your Amazon account login information is needed in order to make any adjustment to these.

Account Settings
Tap here to adjust the account's name, email or password.

Current country
Each Kindle account includes personal information such as your country. If you relocate abroad, the Current Country setting should be updated. This will allow you to connect with the appropriate Amazon marketplace and other websites. Making the change should take no more than a half hour.

Payment Options
You can modify the 1-Click Payment setting to enter a new credit or debit card. Remember to modify not just the Amazon store payment setting, but your ongoing Kindle subscriptions as well, if you have any.

Subscriptions
Any subscriptions you might have, including Magazine and Blog subscriptions, can be found and administered here.

Social Network Accounts
Your device is able to sync with Facebook and Twitter accounts. Press the Facebook or Twitter icons and the respective sites will ask you to log in to your account.

Help (Amazon Assist)

This setting will take you to Amazon Assist, the device's support resource. It includes Mayday, the latest support tool (details below), and numerous other troubleshooting resources on the system.

Mayday

Mayday is the latest user support tool from Amazon. It is designed to make the HDX experience engaging and enjoyable. It also offers support for the Amazon marketplace.

Press the yellow Connect button to turn Mayday on. An Amazon support consultant will appear in no more than 15 seconds (as stated by Amazon themselves). This person will be able to view what is on your screen in order to address your questions and resolve your issues as quickly as possible. The consultant will be visible to you, but not visa-versa.

Mayday provides support 24 hours a day, 7 days a week, 365 days a year. A weak wireless connection can make the service less effective. As of right now, English is the only support staff language

More Features of Amazon Assist

Underneath the Mayday icon are three more options: wireless, user guide and contact us.

Choose wireless to view the steps necessary to establish Wi-Fi and/or Bluetooth connections. You will also find step-by-step assistance with network connectivity issues.

Choose the User Guide to view a more condensed version of this guide. This will be helpful as a quick reference.

Swipe across the screen to the right or press the icon on the upper left of the Amazon Assist screen to open a navigation panel. In addition to the above-mentioned features, you will also be able to view some general controls.

Parental Controls

Next listed are the settings for parental controls. This is a little misleading because both controls for children and all users are found in this section.

This section is divided into two sub-sections: 8 and under, and 9 and up. Choose the 8 and under option and you will be directed to one of the latest Amazon apps called Kindle FreeTime. Here you can set-up user profiles that provide you the capabilities to restrict access to content only recommended for children between the ages of 3 and 8.

The controls for those 9 and up (every other user) can be found underneath the Kindle FreeTime icon. These manage

HDX operations in their entirety, including purchasing, content filtering, Internet settings and more.

Kindle FreeTime

Let's first examine the controls for those of younger ages by looking at Kindle Free Time, a parental controls app for controlling the user experience for young children.

Begin by pressing the icon and going to the FreeTime registration page. You will be able to create a new account.

To create standard profiles, hit the Get Started button on the bottom of the Kindle FreeTime home screen. Type in the Parental Controls Password (or create a new one if you haven't done so yet). After the password is set you will be prompted to add a profile for any children if you wish.

The Add Child Profile page lets you specify name, age and gender of the child the profile is for. You can also pick a cute picture as an identifier for the profile. After you have entered this information, hit Next. This will take you to the Manage Content & Subscription page and the user profile that is now complete.

Tap on the profile to see what media is viewable for that profile. To see all content on your HDX (regardless of profiles), use the dropdown box to click on "All."

While within a profile, you will find alongside each media file there is a box you may check/un-check to allow or restrict viewing of the file for that profile. After scanning the content and determining which to restrict, hit the "Done" button on the upper right of the display. This will return you to the Subscription page. This page shows how the number of files for each media type that profile is allowed to view.

Return to the previous page (Add Child Profile) if you want to generate more profiles. If not, tap the home button.

To switch profiles on your device and allow a child to use it, go to the Kindle FreeTime App and select the corresponding profile. Only the content you've approved for that profile will now appear until the parental controls password is entered once more upon exiting Kindle FreeTime.

Additional Subscription

Amazon offers a premium subscription service, FreeTime Unlimited, which comes preloaded media, games, and books for children 3 – 8. This service is recommended as an effective way to create a user profile with content that has already been vetted for this age group. New content is added all the time, but there is a monthly price associated with opting into this service.

Additional Controls

With FreeTime profiles now arranged, you will want to adjust your controls for those users utilizing the full suite of the HDX's offerings and not restricted to a FreeTime profile.

From within Parental Controls, you can locate these settings listed under the FreeTime app. Toggling these controls on you will prompt creation of a password. Put it in twice and then hit Submit.

Once these Parental Controls are activated you will see a lock on the Status Bar. Tap on the lock to turn the controls off or on. When activated, web browsing, email/contacts/calendars utilities, social media sharing, and camera use can all be controlled.

Additionally, there are some other very important controls you can adjust including the ability to purchase content. You will certainly want to password protect many of these capabilities if other users will be using your device:

Password Protection Purchases: Ability to make purchases with the Amazon Shop application or at the Amazon Store

Password Protection Video Playback: Ability to view a video

Change Password: Ability to change the parental controls password

Password Protect Wi-Fi: Ability to enable Wi-Fi

Password Protect LBS: Ability to enable Location-Based Services

Block and Unblock Content Types: Hit this button to open a screen that displays the full range of content types: Newsstand, Books & Audiobooks, Music, Video, Docs, Apps & Games, and Photos. You can mark each of them as blocked or unblocked.

Hit the back button to go back to Parental Controls setting.

Device

Information and hardware data relating to your HDX can be found in the Device setting section. You can view/manage the following:

The Battery Meter – Shows what % of your device's battery life remains.

Show Battery Percentage in Status Bar – Enable this feature to show the battery indicator in the status bar. Turn it off to hide the indicator.

Your System Updates – Click here to see what system updates are available. You will see a "check now" button. Once you choose this option you will see the newest updates (if there are any). Tap the ones you want to be applied to your device. Check this page periodically as the latest updates will continue to come out.

Your Language – Click here to choose which language you would like your device to operate in. You will have a number of options to choose from.

Text-to-Speech – The HDX offer this features, which reads books aloud to the user. Choose the language and voice you would like enabled.

The Date And Time – Set your device's date and time here. Pick the appropriate time zone and the HDX will do the rest. You can also enable/un-enable the 24-hour time display feature from this page.

Your Storage – You can view the amount of your HDX's drive space being taken up by your media files. Click on any of the 12 categories to see the full listing of your saved files. Tap on any of the individual files to delete them.

Enable ADB – Your HDX comes with this feature disabled as a security precaution. It is meant for application development purposes and will leave your data exposed.

Your Serial Number – Listed here in case you need it for purchase or warranty purposes.

Reset to Factory Defaults – Tap here to make your settings go back to their original factory versions. This can be useful if you are having trouble undoing a problematic setting change. WARNING: Performing this function will erase your personal information as well as the content you have downloaded.

Wireless

The following wireless features can be adjusted in this section:

Airplane Mode

Enable Airplane Mode while flying if necessary. You will not have a wireless connection while it is enabled. A small airplane will appear in upper right corner of the status bar. Tap the button again to turn it back off.

Wi-Fi

You can toggle the Wi-Fi button on this page to turn it on or off. Available wireless networks will appear beneath the button when it is enabled. Choose which one you want to connect to and type in the password if required.

Bluetooth

Toggle the Bluetooth feature on or off from here. When it is enabled, you can see a list of devices your own device can connect to.

An icon that looks like an antenna will show up on your Status Bar when Bluetooth is enabled. Now you can connect wirelessly to keyboards, controller, A2DP compatible headsets, speakers and headphones.

Location-Based Services

When you enable this you will see an alert that says, "By enabling this feature, location data about your Kindle is sent to Amazon and third-party apps and websites…" Tap "Continue" to allow this.

Doing so will make your physical location available to external web-based tools that can streamline your searches based on localized options, saving you the time of refining them yourself. To shut this off, simply press the button once more.

Applications

For more intricate controls and information, the settings for every app on your device can be found in this section.

Apps from Unknown Sources

This controls you're ability to download apps from outside the Amazon App Store. Doing so may put your device at a security risk so be sure to only use apps that come from a trusted source. It is not recommended that you do this unless you are an experienced user / app developer.

Collect App Usage Data

Enable this feature to allow Amazon to compile data on your application usage history. You will receive purchasing suggestions that follow past purchases when this is on. Leaving it off will not otherwise have any affect on your user experience.

Manage All Applications

In addition to downloaded apps, your device also comes with system applications for essential operations, which are listed here. Clicking on any of them will prompt a page with information like App name, memory requirement, cache captured and permissions.

The "Force Stop" function can be used here. It will cause the selected application to cease running immediately. It is best to consult with an Amazon agent via your Mayday connection before using this function yourself.

Notifications & Quiet Time

Quiet Time

You can manage the Quiet Time feature as well as the notification settings in this section.

Press the Quiet Time button to access this function.

Temporary Quiet Time
Enable or Un-enable this feature here or in the Quick Settings menu.

Scheduled Quiet Time
Quiet Time can be set to turn on while you are engaged in certain activities:
Viewing TV or movies, reading books, magazines or newspapers, listening to audiobooks or MP3s, or Browsing in Silk. Click on the checkbox next to the activity of choice.

Turn on Quiet Time on a schedule each day
You can select a specific time of day for Quiet Time to activate here.

Notifications

Underneath Quiet Time is a complete listing of apps. Click on any of them to view the corresponding notification settings.

You have the option of making the app's notifications appear/not appear. You can also turn off or on the setting for a sound to be played in conjunction with a notification.

Display & Sounds

Volume

The volume bar can be slid up or down to control volume on your HDX. The volume controls on the back can do this as well.

Notification Sound
This setting allows you to pick a default sound for your device. A display of sound options is available.

Auto Brightness
This feature can also be enabled from the quick settings menu and allows your device to adjust the brightness automatically based on the environment you are in and the application being used at the time.

Display Brightness
If you want to control the brightness on your display manually, use the slider here.

Display Mirroring

If your device is Miracast-compatible, you will be able to recreate your screen display on another device's screen (mirroring), such as an HD TV. Audio will also transfer to the other device.

Without this compatibility, you can still mirror wirelessly to the other device by putting an HDMI adapter on it. Recommended: the NETGEAR Push2TV Wireless Display HDMI Adapter – Miracast and WiDi (PTV3000) http://www.amazon.com/gp/product/B00904JILO/.

How To Enable Mirroring

To enable mirroring, the device you want your HDX to connect to must be "discoverable" via wireless signal. Settings to make a device discoverable can be different for each of them and you might need to refer to the device's own user guide for instructions.

Once discoverable, swipe downward on your screen to get to the Quick Settings menu and go to the settings page. Go to the Display & Sounds menu and then Display Mirroring. The HDX should then find all discoverable devices in range. Choose the one you want to connect to and then hit Connect.

In no more than 20 seconds your HDX will be mirrored with the other device, on which you should be able to see and hear the same things you do on the HDX. This can also be confirmed if the word "mirroring" appears beneath your HDX's name. You can press Stop Mirroring to disconnect.

Display Sleep

Tap on Display Sleep to go to a page for selecting the amount of inactivity time you would like to lapse before your device automatically goes into sleep mode. The sooner it enters this mode, the more power you will save.

Keyboards

Use the Keyboards settings to control the digital keyboard that comes up on your display when you need to type.

Languages

Click here to choose which language you would like your keyboard to operate in. You will have a number of options to choose from. To choose a default language, go to Tap on Default Language and pick your language of choice.

Hit the Download Languages button to view a larger list online and download the one you want. This can be made your Default Language if you like.

Keyboard Settings

Sounds on Key Press – Enable/Un-enable sounds while typing on the keyboard.

Auto Correction – Enable/Un-Enable the feature that automatically corrects your spelling errors.

Auto Capitalization – Enable/Un-enable for automatically correcting capitalization errors.

Next word prediction – This feature uses your typing history to automatically offer complete words before you finish typing them.

Check Your Spelling – This feature marks spelling mistakes.

Your Personal Dictionary – Words you use a lot will show up at the top of your screen. You can click on them to save them in you Personal Dictionary. The complete list of selected words is found here. Words can also be removed from the dictionary in this view with the "Delete" button.

Bluetooth Keyboard

Here you can view the Bluetooth keyboard settings if you have connected your device to one.

You can choose the default keyboard language and you can access a listing of the keyboard shortcuts the Bluetooth keyboard offers, allowing you to type faster.

Accessibility

These features can detect specific types of hand motions and provide audible responses to your activities on HDX. These are customized tools that have been designed to meet the needs of a small percentage of HDX users. Setting them up requires a tutorial:

Security

The HDX can be set up with Lock Screen so that every time you attempt to use the device after it has fallen asleep, you will have to enter a four-digit PIN.

Press the Lock Screen button and create your PIN. You will be required to enter it a second time to confirm it. Then hit Finish.

Once you have logged-in with your PIN, you will have the option to change the four-digit code. You can also adjust how often the Lock Screen feature will go into effect. The device is originally set to go to Lock Screen whenever the HDX goes into sleep mode.

Credential Storage And Device Administrators

Both of these settings are meant for enterprise applications rather than consumer usage.

Legal & Compliance

You can view legal/compliance information pertaining to your HDX in any one of these categories: Legal Notices, Terms of Use, Safety & Compliance and Privacy. The information can vary from country to country and you may need to identify which country you are in.

Keep in mind, the information in these sections is not the complete legal documentation but an overview and a link to Amazon's full documentation.

Downloading, Syncing, and Sending

Amazon's Cloud Services & Your HDX

The Amazon Cloud will be the primary platform from which you acquire and manage your media library.

Cloud services in particular is a reference to the storage space Amazon provides you with via their website, so that your device is not overloaded and you won't need to rely on your own external storage device(s).

Amazon provides as much space for your Amazon Purchased media as you need. It also provides 5GB of storage for non-Amazon Purchased files. These are free with your device, and additional space for non-Amazon Purchased files can be bought (most users will never need additional space).

You can set-up your Amazon media library so that your device contains all the same files as your cloud library. Since your cloud has unlimited storage capacity but your device does not, it is recommended that you only store files on your device that you plan on viewing in the near future.

Finding Your Cloud's Content on Your HDX

Your device's content libraries have tabs to display your local media files (On Device) and those stored in the cloud (Cloud). When you view from the Cloud tab you will be shown all of your content.

Sync Your Cloud and HDX Content

With a Wi-Fi connection established, you have the ability to synchronize content between your cloud and your device. In addition to the media files themselves syncing, so to will your viewing/reading progress within them. That means that TV shows you've watched on the cloud can be resumed in place from your HDX.

Sync All Content

To sync all of your Amazon Cloud content with the Cloud content on the HDX, use the Sync All Content feature. From the Home screen, pull up the Quick Settings menu by swiping down the display. Select Sync All Content. Keep in mind, doing so will sync content, but it will not automatically download from the Amazon to your device. This must be done separately.

Download Individual Items From Cloud

To select individual files to move from your Amazon Cloud to your device for local storage and usage, make sure you have a Wi-Fi connection and go to the Home screen. Choose the Kindle content library where the media file is located and click on the file. If the file has been downloaded to your device previously the box to the right of its icon will be checked. If there is no check, tap it and it will then download.

Transfer Via USB

Media files can be moved from your computer to your HDX by connecting the two devices using the micro-USB cable. The cable plugs in to the USB ports on both the HDX and the computer you wish to transfer from.

On Mac computers you will need to download an app to enable this process: Kindle.com/support/downloads. Windows users must have the most up-to-date Windows Media Player.

Once you've don this, and the devices are connected, you will have access to an HDX folder as seen from your computer. Simply click and drag the media files you wish to move from your computer into the folder.

These file formats are compatible with your device:

Audiobooks: AAX, AA
Books: MOBI, AZW (.azw3), KF8
Documents: TXT, PDF, PRC, DOCX, DOC
Music: E-AC-3 (Dolby Digital Plus), AC-3 (Dolby Digital), MP3,
AAC (.m4a), OGG, MIDI, MP4, WAV, AAC LC/LTP, HE-
AACv2, HE-AACv1, AMR-WB, AMR, NB
Pictures: JPEG, GIF, PNG, BMP
Movies: MP4, 3GP, VP8 (with video playback at 720p)

Removing Content

Remove Your Content From Device

To free up room for new media files on your device, you
should move older files off of it. On the settings screen, select
Device and then Storage. A categorized menu of your media
library will come up. Each category displays the file list within,
as well as storage space. Select a file by clicking on its
checkbox and then hit "Remove from HDX." You will still have
the file stored in your Amazon Cloud library.

Remove Your Content From Cloud (Not Recommended)

Deleting files from your Amazon Cloud library will mean they
are completely gone from any and all storage places provided
by your Amazon account and devices.

While in your Amazon Cloud library, tap and hold a file and the
option for "Delete from Cloud" will appear.

Make sure the file is saved on a separate removable drive or
in another cloud-based storage solution if you want to be able
to access it in the future.

Your Send-to-Kindle Email

Every HDX comes with a "Send-to-Kindle" email address to which new media files can be sent and added to the device/cloud library by email delivery. The emails must come from approved addresses.

The address can be found in your Amazon account under "Manage Your Devices."

Send Documents

Once you have identified your "Send-to-Kindle" email, go to the Personal Document Settings page, also from the Manage Your Devices tab.

Add email addresses from which you would like to receive new media files and they will be marked as safe senders for Send-to-Kindle purposes.

Senders do not need to include anything in the subject line of their messages to your Send-to-Kindle address. But if they put "convert" in the subject line, Amazon will automatically convert from PDF to Amazon format (.azw). This way you will be able to adjust font size, add annotations and use Whispersync.

These added files sync with your Amazon Cloud library just as any other file would. You can choose to turn this automatic syncing off from the Personal Document Settings page. Amazon allots 5 gigabytes of storage for non-Amazon purchased content without additional charges. You can buy more storage if you wish. Also note that there are fees for these file transfers when done without the use of Wi-Fi.

Additional Information:

To keep up on Amazon's newest changes to this feature, please visit: http://amzn.to/1csW43W

Send-To-Kindle Application

Go to http://www.amazon.com/gp/sendtokindle to download
the Send-To-Kindle app to your computer.

This feature lets you add personal files from computers,
mobile devices and cloud storage to your Kindle with one
simple click. The files will automatically be formatted for Kindle
compatibility and will be ready for use right away.

Amazon Prime

What is Amazon Prime?

Members of the Amazon Prime package have 41,000+ TV and movie titles to chose from to be streamed directly to their device. Kindle Books from a library of 350,000+ can be borrowed and read, one per month and 2-day shipping on product orders is also included.

All of this is included for a current annual membership cost of $79.00 (subject to change). All new HDX owners will get a complimentary month of Amazon Prime with their device.

Your HDX can also play media from Amazon's extensive media library. While browsing, you can download items of interest and view them later, even without an Internet connection. Your device can be your all-in-one solution for media storage, management and viewing enjoyment!

Borrowing Books for Free From the Kindle Owners' Lending Library

Amazon Prime membership includes one book per month. The Kindle Lending Library contains 350,000+ titles to chose from. This includes popular series like Harry Potter and Hunger Games, and works from award-winning writers like Kurt Vonnegut.

Browse Your Kindle Owners Lending Library

Members can reach the Lending Library by going to the Home screen and selecting "Shop" and then "Books" from the side menu. Use the icon with three horizontal lines on top of each other in the top left of the screen to bring out the Navigation Panel. Chose "Kindle Lending Library" and you have made it.

To check-out a book for your free monthly rental, click on it and then chose "Borrow for Free" which can be found beneath the "Buy" tab. This will initiate the download.

Prime Instant Video

Amazon Prime membership includes access to 41,000+ television and movie titles. You can watch hits like Duck Dynasty, Downtown Abbey, Parks & Recreation, SpongeBob SquarePants and Arrested Development as part of your membership fee.

This service also gives you access to thousands of movies, many of which are in high-definition. Popular titles include Marvel's Avengers, The Italian Job, Thor, and Hook, just to name a few. These can be watched online or saved for later, and there is no cap on the number of available titles you can access.

Browse Prime's Instant Video

To view the library of movies and television options in the Amazon Prime library, look in the top left corner of the Home screen and select "Shop." Select "Videos" and you will see the "Recently Added to Prime" options.

If you want to see the full library and not just the new releases, again start at the Home screen and tap on the icon that looks like three horizontal lines stacked on top of each other, located in the top left of the screen. You can chose between "Prime TV Shows" , "Prime Movies" and "For the Kids."

All the titles, recently added or older, can be accessed for free with your membership.

To view a television title, tap on "Prime TV Shows" and choose the show you want. A menu of available seasons/episodes will come up. Within the episode view you can tap into the text section for each episode to pop out a more full description of the episode.

To the right there will be a downward pointing arrow (tap to download) and a play icon (tap to view the episode online).

For downloading- the HDX will let you select the download quality: Best, Better of Good.

"Best" quality will result in a file with 1080p HD. "Better" will be 720p HD and it will take the longest to download and take up the most drive space. "Good" will not have quite as high quality of a picture but it will download quicker and take up little space. However you download, you will be free to run other applications while this occurs.

You can track how much time remains in your download with the "Download in progress" meter. This can be accessed through the Quick Settings menu on your Home screen.

Using The Content Libraries

EBooks Library

Reading Books

You can access your device's Books Library through the Navigation Bar on the Home screen. Select any book in your library and click on it to open it.

Swipe your finger across the screen from right-to-left to turn to the next page of a book. Swipe the opposite way to go back. Tap on any part of the page to open additional reading options: View, X-Ray, Notes, Share and Bookmark. The bottom of the page has a progress meter. The further along you are in the book, the further across the line the dot will be. You can also see what page number you are on and what percentage of the book has been read.

Aa
View   X-Ray   Notes   Share   Bookmarks

take the cash and see what tomorrow brings. Maybe he'd keep the next one to himself for a few days.

Reading Options

"See what ordered Martin Kyle, who was sitting in the passenger seat.

Tap for TOC Tim Garbutt nodded **Bookmarks** current beat and voiced his displeasure when the disc was changed.

"Aww, I was listening to that."

"Stop bleating, Timmy," Kyle said, switching the CD for something with a bit more drum and bass, "my gran wouldn't even listen to that crap."

Boyle laughed, but his eyes were on the black Skoda coming towards them. The thick aerial first caught his attention, and as it neared he saw the white shirts and black epaulettes of the occupants that identified them as police in an unmarked car. The Skoda passed them and in his rear view mirror he watched it continue for another hundred yards before the blue lights illuminated and it performed a u-turn.

Game on.

Click & Drag to Navigate

* * *

Skip ahead multiple pages in the book by pressing down on the dot on the progress meter and sliding it to the right. This isn't an exact science but it will save time. Slide the dot left to skip back multiple pages.

Navigating the Table of Contents

Regardless of what page you are on in the book, the Table of Contents menu can be accessed by tapping any spot on the display (you won't lose your place in the book). There is an icon with three horizontal lines on top of each other in the top left of the screen. Press on it and the "Table of Contents" section with all the chapters will come up. Click on the one you want to view.

To skip ahead/back with more accuracy than sliding the progress meter ball, pull up the "Go to Page or Location" feature on the same menu as the "Table of Contents." This will prompt a search bar and electronic keyboard. Type in the page number and select "Page" or type in the location and select "Location" to go where you want to go.

Changing Text Size

Press on any spot on the book display. On the upper left you will see the "View" button. This feature will allow you to adjust font size, background color, spacing and margins.

Changing Background Color

The background color can be changed from the second row in the View menu. Slide the "T" icon left to make the background lighter and to the right to make it darker and ultimately black. The text will automatically change to white if the background is black. When the icon is in the center, the background will be a color called "Sepia."

Changing Margin Size

Underneath the Change Background Color tool is the tool for adjusting the size of the margins. Press the icon on the left of the screen to shrink the page margins and the one on the right to make them bigger. The center icon makes the margins mid-sized. Smaller margins allow more room for text and vice-versa.

Changing Line Spacing

Underneath the Change Margin Size tool is the tool for changing the size of the spaces between the lines of text. The icon with the three horizontal lines closest together makes the space between lines of text the smallest. The icon with the three horizontal lines furthest apart will make the space the largest.

Changing Fonts

Underneath the tool for Changing Line Spacing there is a tool for adjusting the font style (Times New Roman, Arial, Calibri, etc.). Tap on the tool and a list of available font styles will appear. Tap on the one you want to use.

Tap twice on any spot on the display to access the Book Menu. The "X-Ray" feature is to the left of "Notes." The X-Ray feature provides extra details about the story you are in, including "People" which will tell you about the characters and "Terms" which will elaborate on some of the terms used, places involved or other information useful to the reader. Select "All" to view both. You can click through to a Wikipedia article for even more information.

Taking Notes While Reading

From the reading view, press on any spot on the screen and a menu will come up. Tap "Notes."
From this view you can create and save Notes and Marks while you are reading.

To add a new note, tap "X" in the top right of the menu. Now tap on the page and select "Note." You can see previously entered notes and can also use the electronic keyboard/text bar to enter the new information. Tap "Save" when you are done.

Adding Bookmarks While Reading

Just like old-fashioned paper bookmarks you may have used to save your place within a printed book, Amazon eBooks have an electronic bookmark feature. Press down on the screen on the page you would like to save. Select "Bookmarks" on the top right and then "Add Bookmark."

Multiple bookmarks can be created within one book. When you select "Bookmarks" to add a new one, you will also see previously-created bookmarks. Tap on any of these to jump to the page in the book it is saving.

You can delete a bookmark from the "Bookmarks" menu by tapping on the one you wish to delete and selecting "Remove Bookmark" from the top of the menu that comes up.

Text-to-Speech For Books

Many books on Amazon can be read to you by your device using the Text-to-Speech feature. A "Play" button will appear on the display if it is available for the book your are reading.

You can adjust the voice used in this feature. From the Home page, swipe downward toward the bottom of the display and the Quick Settings menu will come up. Choose "Settings" then

"Device" and then "Default Voice." The majority of HDXs provide a voice with an Australian accent or an American accent. Move the dot to the one you prefer.

There are more voice types for you to choose from and download. Skip back from the "Default Voice" view and then tap on "Download Additional Voice." Press on any voice you want to add and after it is downloaded it will appear on the "Default Voice" view.

Taking Out Library Books

HDX users can rent books electronically from thousands of resources across the world wide web outside of the Amazon library.

An application called Overdrive must be downloaded to your HDX to use this feature. Overdrive lets you manage the books you are streaming and will remove them from the device once your rental period has run out. Download here: http://search.overdrive.com

Many municipal libraries will let you rent books electronically. You will need to contact your nearest libraries and set up an account with them if you have not already done so. After an account is established, go to the Amazon home page and view the Public Library Loan page. After you tap on your book of choice, all of your Amazon-linked devices will appear. Choose the device you want to read the book on and tap "Get library book."

EBooks From Other Sites

Amazon has a larger book selection than any other marketplace. It is not the only one of course. Electronic books from other services can be bought and downloaded to your HDX as well.

Make sure the eBook files you download are compatible with your device. The following formats will work:

- **MOBI**
- **KF8**
- **AZW**
- **PRC**

eBooks can also be downloaded and stored in your "Docs" folder, which may help you avoid the above compatibility issues.

Project Gutenberg

There are 42,000+ electronic books available in the public domain at no cost, many of them time-honored classics. Project Gutenberg's goal is to help a larger audience access these works.

Nearly all of these titles are Kindle-compatible. A MOBI format may be used on your device as well. Visit: http://www.gutenberg.org/ and select a book to download. Once complete, go to the "Downloads" tab in your web browser to access it.

Newsstand – Magazines & Newspapers

Your favorite magazines can now be accessed on your device. The latest issues will be immediately available to you electronically as soon as they hit the newsstands!

Purchasing Magazines

You can access magazines and newspapers via the Home screen by tapping "Shop" on the Navigation Bar. Swipe through the carousel to view magazine subscriptions that are trending the most, or peruse other popular subscriptions displayed below it. Swipe upwards to view offers like "First 30 Days Free" and "Featured Deals on Kindle Magazines."

Click on the icon that looks like a magnifying glass in the top right of the screen to search for a specific magazine subscription that you are interested in.

Magazine & Newspaper Listing Page

Tap on a magazine to view more details on its listing and description page. You will have the option to "Subscribe now" if this is a new magazine for you. Beneath the Subscribe now tab you can choose between buying an individual issue or an Annual subscription. After making this choice, the HDX will start downloading.

Verifying Subscriptions

If the magazine is one you have an existing subscription for, you should be able to transfer it and access the electronic version as well. Press "Verify your subscription" from the Listing Page. Entering your account number is the first and simplest option for account verification. This number should be on any one of your paper versions of the magazine. Enter the number into the "Subscription account number" box. Enter your zip code in the appropriate box as well.

An HDX version of this account must now be created, with a username and password. Afterward, the most recent issue will start downloading.

NOTE: Many publications provide content as applications instead of electronic issues. These applications will have many of the same articles, but will also include more interactive features and some unique content. Where applications are available, your device will automatically redirect you to the App store when you attempt to make the purchase.

Reading Magazines

The Home page's Navigation Bar has an option called "Newsstand." When you tap on it, all the issues you saved locally will display as "On Device." Other issues associated with your Amazon account that were purchased on different devices may also appear in the "Cloud" tab.

The icon with three horizontal lines on top of each other will take you to a selection of Newsstand categories in the Amazon Store.

Magazine Navigation

Press down on a magazine to pull it up. The navigation process is much like that of an eBook's, simply slide your finger across the screen from right to left to advance to the next page. You can also scan up and down within a page by sliding your finger.

Tap on any place in the display to prompt the Table of Contents menu. This will present the different articles within the issue that you may skip ahead to. To exit the menu, slide your finger outside of the menu like you are turning a page and you will return to the magazine.

Tap on any place in the display and then choose "Browse" in the top right of the screen if you would like to peruse the magazine from a higher level. Press any part of the display near the bottom to go back.

Bookmark Magazines

Bookmarks can be inserted to keep your place in magazines just as they can in eBooks. While in the reading view, press on any place in the page and then choose Bookmarks. From here you are able to skip forward/back to bookmarks, as well as remove bookmarks or create new ones.

Music

You can play music on your device's built-in speakers with excellent sound quality thanks to Dolby Digital Plus, which has numerous features enhancing your listening experience. You can also plug-in headphones or connect it to another player.

Shopping for Music on Amazon

As you may have guessed, Amazon has a large selection of music to browse. While on the Home screen, press "Shop" and then "Music" to reach the Amazon Music Store.

You can scan through the carousel to view promotions and deals and to search for music by category. Underneath the carousel will be a best sellers menu you can scan through. There are more categories further down the page.

You can search for a specific song, album or artist while in the Amazon Music Store by tapping the icon that looks like a magnifying glass in the top right portion of the screen. This will bring up a keyboard and search bar to type the search details into. Press "Cancel" to return.

You can also view music categories by tapping the icon with three horizontal lines on top of each other in the top left of the screen. The Navigation Panel that comes up will have the "Shop" option. Tap here to view categories like "Best Sellers", "New Releases", "Browse Genres" and "Gift Cards & Promotions".

Purchasing Music

If you would like to buy an album from the Amazon Music store, tap its icon and you will go to its listing page.

Songs on an album can be bought individually. Tap the small yellow box alongside the song you are interested in to view its cost. On the other side of the icon is the "Play" button which will let you listen to a short clip of the song.

If you would like to buy the entire album, tap the "Buy Album" button at the top. Typically, the price of a complete album is less than the price of purchasing each track individually.

From the album listing view, swipe downward to pull up the "Customers Also Bought" page to see other artists/albums that might be of interest to you, as well as listener reviews.

Music Store Settings

While inside the Amazon Music Store, use the icon with the three horizontal lines on top of each other to access "Settings." You can enable/un-enable "Automatic Downloads" from here. If Automatic Downloads is on, all songs added to your cloud library will automatically be downloaded to your HDX. Press "Clear Cache" to clear out your cached songs. Doing so will give you more storage in your music folder.

Adding Your Own Music

Moving songs from your computer's music library onto your device is simple. Connect the two using the USB cable provided and follow the below steps (depending on the type of computer you have) so that file transfer will be enabled:

Mac: Visit Kindle.com/support/downloads to download the "Android File Transfer" app to your computer.

In the "Android File Transfer" program on the computer you can view all the HDX folders. Click and drag the music file/folder from your computer into the appropriate HDX music folder within the program.

When finished, the two devices can be disconnected by opening a file manager a choosing "Eject Android File Transfer" and then detaching the USB cable.

Windows XP: Ensure that the most up-to-date Windows Media Player is on your computer.

Once this is confirmed, open the "My Computer" folder where you will see the USB drive. Drag and drop music files from your computer into this drive and they will transfer to the HDX. When you are done making transfers, close the drive from within the folder before physically disconnecting the two devices.

You can now play the music you transferred on your HDX by going to the Home screen and then choosing "Music" and then "On Device."

Playlists

You can create a playlist on your device with ease. This will allow you to play selected songs from different albums in the order of your choice.

Building a Playlist

Build a new playlist by going into the Music Library on your device. Press the icon with three horizontal lines on top of each other and then press "Playlists." The "Cloud" list will only include artists and songs that are saved in your Amazon Cloud. The "On Device" list will only include artists and songs saved on the HDX.

Press the "+" icon on the top right of the display. The electronic keyboard will come up. Give the playlist a title and then press "Save." You can now search for tracks in your library to put on your list. When you see one you want, press the yellow "+" button next to it. To take it back off the list, press the "-" button.

Once you have all the tracks you want, tap on the "Done" button in the top right of your screen. The playlists can be altered at any time.

Playing Your Playlist

Press "Play All" to start playing a list. From here you are able to pause, skip, shuffle tracks or go back a track.

Adding Songs & Deleting Playlists

As you come across songs in your library you would like to add to a playlist, tap down and hold on it. Tap "Add to playlist" when the prompt comes up. Choose which one of your playlists you would like to put in on and you're done.

A playlist can be deleted by tapping and holding down on it until the prompt comes up with the "Remove from Device" option. Choose this option and the playlist will be gone, but the songs will remain in your library.

Audiobooks

The HDX can play audiobooks as well. To browse available audiobooks, go to the home screen and tap "Shop" in the main menu. Choosing "Audiobooks" will take you to the Audiobooks Store. Here you can navigate popular titles or search for a particular title you are interested in. Every selection has a "Play Sample" feature underneath it. Tap on this to hear a short sample of the book. Tap it once more to end the sample play.

Purchasing Audiobooks

You can buy an audiobook by tapping on it and pressing "Buy" on the listing page that will come up. Credit card information may be required for those without Audible.com accounts.

Listening to Audiobooks

After it has downloaded, play the audiobook by pressing "Listen Now." The following options will come up on the lower left part of the display: Go back (in 30 second increments); Pause; Insert a bookmark. Much like with traditional eBooks, you can add a note as well by pressing down and holding on the page which you wish to leave the note for.

Icons for these options will appear on the lower right part of the display: Sleep timer; Adjust the narration speed; Adjust volume. Pressing the icon with the three horizontal lines on top of each other on the top right of your display will bring up a Table of Contents. From here you can select a chapter to skip to. You can also see your saved bookmarks in the top right of the screen and skip to any of them.

Audiobook Library

Open the Audiobook Library by tapping "Audiobooks" in the menu in the topmost portion of your Home screen. This will take you to a grid-like display of the audiobooks you have saved in the cloud and on the HDX.

Whispersync

The Amazon "Whispersync" feature will synch any books for which you have downloaded both the audio and eBook versions. Some books do not include this feature. Books that have it will say "Whispersync for Voice" in their listing page.

Audible

After purchasing an audiobook on Amazon, an "Audible" account in your name will instantly be generated. "Audible" will help you manage your device's audiobook library. Your account can be accessed on Audible.com with the same username and password.

Apps & Games

Your device has an assortment of widely used apps and hit games (most can be downloaded without charge). To browse Amazon's App store, press "Shop" in the top left part of the Home screen. Press "Apps" and you will be in the Store. "Featured Apps and Games," and "Recommended For You Based on Your Book Interests" are two of the many categories you can use to help you find the right book.

The carousel at the topmost part of the screen has promotions like "Free App of the Day." Press any of these to view the details.

While on a category of interest in the main app store view, you can swipe through different apps that fall under that category. Use the icon that looks like a magnifying glass on the top right of the screen to pull up a search box/keyboard and enter the name of a particular app you want.

Downloading & Purchasing Apps

To see the cost and other purchasing details for an app, press and hold on its icon (free apps will say "Free" in lieu of a price). Users rate many of these apps, and you can see the average number of stars they award to it. The number next to the stars tells you how many ratings have been given.

You can swipe through various screenshot of the app underneath the price bar. Press on any of them to bring up a larger view. Press on the enlarged picture to return to the previous view.

Under the assorted screenshots you can read a short description of the app. "Key Details" can be found to the right.

Apps that are not free can be purchased with credit cards or the Amazon Coin payment system (see the next section).

After downloading, tap "Open" from the listing page to access it.

Amazon Coins

To get the best possible deal on Amazon products, you can purchase Amazon Coins, an online currency used exclusively within Amazon.

One dollar will buy you 100 Amazon Coins. You can buy them in bulk, and the larger quantity you buy the larger the discount will be:

$4.80 is worth 500 Amazon Coins (4% cost reduction). $90 will get you 10,000 coins. This trend continues to go up, saving you more. If you are an Amazon regular, this is a no-brainer!

All HDX devices come with 500 Amazon Coins complimentary. This will give you a good opportunity to try them out. With any Amazon purchase, you can pay with these coins by clicking on the "Amazon Coins" button on the checkout screen.

Test Driving Apps

From an app's listing view, there is a small green bar beneath its icon. Tap on this bar and you will be able to sample the app for a few minutes to see how you like it. There will be a countdown clock on the top left of the screen letting you know how much longer you can sample the app.

When you are done with your sampling of the app, press the "Quit" button on the top left part of the screen. To buy the app, press the yellow button (which will have the price on it) on the top right part of the page.

Purchasing Games

You can buy and download games from Amazon's Game Store using steps very similar to those used to download apps. Press "Shop" in the top left part of the Home screen and then press "Games" to enter the Games store. This is laid out in a format much like the App Store's. Tap on the icon for the game you are interested in to view more information and/or buy it.

GameCircle

Use the GameCircle service to save the progress you have made within a game. In addition to "bookmarking" your progress, GameCircle can also log your scores and other achievements for competition with other gamers.

Video And Photos

Your device is an excellent tool for viewing and storage of videos and photos. The interface is highly dynamic and user-friendly and the screen is high resolution, which makes for a sharp picture with colorful images.

Browsing Photos

While on the Home screen, press "Photos" on the Navigation Bar in the top right part of the display. This will take you to a grid-like display of every photo/video you have taken with the device's camera and any photos/videos you have uploaded or downloaded to it.

Tap a photo or video if you would like to view it. Once in view, there will be three choices:

Posting Photos to Social Media Networks

Press the "Share" icon (3 dots with a line through them) if you want to share a picture or video with friends. You can synch your email, Facebook or Twitter accounts to your HDX and post them on any of these sites. Accounts not already synched will generate a prompt requesting the user ID and password you would normally use for that site. Once synched, you will be able to instantly post on the site.

Sharing Multiple Photos

If you would like to post more than one photo at a time on social media, go to the grid-style view of the entire library. Press the icon with 3 dots with a line through them and then tap on whichever photos you would like to put on the post. Chose the social media site(s) to send them to and you are done.

Editing & Deleting Photos

Your device has numerous photo editing capabilities: Apply stickers; Insert text; Adjust Contrast or Saturation and more. You can even make your photo look like a meme picture.

As you search through your photo library, press any place on the screen to pull up a toolbar at the top. You can View Info, Delete, or Edit the photo you are on.

Editing options are: Enhance, Crop, Rotate, Redeye, Filters, Stickers, Text, Meme, Draw, Brightness, Contrast, Saturation, Warmth, Whiten, Blemish, Sharpness, Focus and Splash. Use "Filters" to add Instagram-like filters to the photo. Tap "Done" when finished.

The Camera Roll feature is another way to view your entire collection of photos in a grid-like display. You can access this feature while a photo is pulled up by tapping any place on the display and then tapping the arrow on the top left of the screen.

Transferring Photos & Video

Transferring photos and video requires connecting your device to a computer with the USB cable that was provided with the device.

Mac users- As with transferring music and eBooks, "Android File Transfer" must be downloaded to your computer. This can be done from this site: http://kindle.com/support/downloads.

Once complete, the program will instantly come up on your computer's screen.

Windows XP users- Must have the most up-to-date version of Windows Media Player to be able to transfer files. If you have it, it will show up as a USB Storage Drive in the "Computer" or "My Computer" folders.

Once you have the appropriate Mac/Windows file transfer program opened, you can view the folders containing all your saved media. Drag the pictures/videos you wish to transfer from your computer into the appropriate media folder by category.

When finished, close the program and disconnect the USB cable.

The following file formats are required for these transfers to work:

For video, the Kindle Fire HDX supports: MP4, 3GP, VP8 (with video playback at 720p)

For photos, the Kindle Fire HDX supports: JPEG, GIF, PNG, BMP

For audio, the Kindle Fire HDX supports: E-AC-3 (Dolby Digital Plus), AC-3 (Dolby Digital), MP3, AAC (.m4a), OGG, MIDI, MP4, WAV, AAC LC/LTP, HE-AACv2, HE-AACv1, AMR-WB, AMR, NB

For documents, the Kindle Fire HDX supports: AZW, PDF, TXT, PRC, DOCX, DOC

Streaming Video from Other Sites

Clips found outside of Amazon can also be streamed on your HDX. Netflix and Hulu are two widely used websites for this, and both have apps available at the Amazon store. They are downloadable at no charge and you can start watching their content right away on your device.

YouTube does not have an app available at the Amazon Store at this time. But you can still watch YouTube content on your HDX by going directly to the YouTube websites.

Documents

While in the Home screen view, press "Docs" to access the Documents Library. This allows you to select a method for transferring documents from your computer to your HDX.

Your options are Email, Sync, Clip and Transfer.

Transferring Docs

The simplest method for moving documents from your computer over to your HDX is to directly transfer them.

Connect your device to your computer using the provided USB cable. For Macs, make sure you have Android File Transfer installed and opened. For Windows users, you need to use Windows file browser.

Click and drag the documents you would like to transfer, and put them in the "Documents" folder on your HDX. When you are in the Documents Library, the documents you transfer will appear in the on-device tab unless they were also saved in the cloud.

Emailing documents is also an easy process. Email the document(s) of your choosing to your Kindle email address and it will automatically show up in the Documents Library.

Syncing Docs with Amazon Cloud

To synch documents with your Amazon Cloud drive, simply press "Sync" and then "Email me install links." You will be sent a weblink. Click through and download the Amazon Cloud Drive app for your desktop. After installation, documents put on your Amazon Cloud will automatically be accessible on your device.

Send-to-Kindle (Clip Articles)

Add the "Send-to-Kindle" feature to your computer to efficiently transfer articles, blog posts and other content to your HDX. You can do this by pressing "Clip" in your Doc Library. Then press "Email me install links." A weblink will be sent to your Amazon email account. Click through and follow the website's instructions to download. After this is complete, choose the device you would like the articles sent to.

Reading & Editing Documents

You can read documents on Kindle in much the same way as you read eBooks. Turning pages requires the same left-to-right swipe of the finger. Tap any place within the page to see options like format change or adding notes/bookmarks. You are able to skip ahead or back in the document with the little ball on the screen's bottom.

You can view or edit files in the ".doc" or ".docx" format. Within the Documents Library, pull up a .doc file by pressing on it. Scroll up/down or left/right to navigate. "Pinch" the screen with two fingers to zoom out, or reverse the motion ("un-pinch") to zoom back in.

OfficeSuite Pro is required software for editing documents on the HDX. This typically costs $14.99. If this is ready, press "Edit" in the toolbar at the top of the page and you are ready to edit.

The Search feature in the document can be accessed by tapping on "Find" in the top right of the display. Type in the word(s) you want to find in the document and it will take you to all the section where they are found. When you are finished, hit "Done."

Printing Documents

If you would like to print a document you have open, press "Print" at the top of the screen to view network printers. The HDX is capable of printing wirelessly as long as your printer of choice can too.

Note: Downloading an app onto your device that is specific to the model of printer you are using may be required. You will be prompted if this is the case.

Browsing the Web

The default web browser for the HDX is "Silk," a speedy and reliable browser that is known to be user-friendly.

You can open a browser by from the Home screen by swiping upward. This will put you in Grid View. Press the Silk icon and a browser will open, allowing you to surf the internet. The websites you visit most frequently will come up, allowing you to navigate to them quickly.

Silk uses tabs for browsing, which lets you visit multiple websites within one browser. Press the "+" button on the top right of the screen and a new tab will come up. You can go to different tabs/sites in a browser by pressing on the desired tab at the top. Pressing the (X) in a tab will close it out.

Full Screen Mode & Navigation

If you would like to make the website you are visiting fill your entire display, press the full-screen button near the bottom. This button looks like a box with arrows pointing up/down/left/right.

You can open a Navigation Panel from within a web page by pressing the button that is square with parallel lines within it. This feature allows you to post the page on social media or email it. "Request Another View" lets you open the web page as a mobile page or a desktop page.

Use the icon with three horizontal lines on top of each other to see the Most Visited sites, Bookmarks, Downloads, and History. The History list has the sites you have visited most recently, newest on top. You can refine the list to sites visited "Today" ; "Yesterday" or "Last 7 days."

Bookmarking a Webpage

You can keep track of websites you have been visiting and/or want to be able to jump back to quickly by bookmarking them.

While on a site, tap down and hold its tab until a menu comes up. Select "Add to Bookmarks." You will be able to edit its name (changing location is also possible but should not be done). Press "OK" and this website will be in your bookmarks.

You can pull up all your bookmarks by tapping the icon with three horizontal lines on top of each other and then "Bookmarks." Your bookmarks will be displayed in a grid view. You can set the view according to Last Accessed, Title, or Number of Visits. To view your bookmarks in list format, press the icon that has four vertical lines on the top right of the screen.

Web pages can be added to your Bookmarks manually by pressing "Add" on the top right of the screen. Type in the page's name and title and press "OK."

Press down one time on a bookmark and it will be opened in your current browser. Tap down and hold on it, and you can choose to pull it up in a new tab, share it, copy the URL, or edit/delete it.

Sharing Bookmarks

Tap down and hold on a bookmark if you would like to show the page to others. You have the option to send it as a link in email or post it on social media. This can all be done with one tap if the accounts are linked to your device.

Trending Now

Press "Trending Now" in the sidebar and you will arrive at a tab containing articles relating to entertainment, sports and other news categories that are getting the most hits currently. The articles are typically drawn from big-name news organizations like CNN, NY Times and Yahoo. You can switch between list view and grid view by using the boxes on the top right of the screen.

Browser Settings

You can adjust your device's browser settings by tapping on the button in the top left of your screen, which will prompt the sidebar. Press "Settings." Note that the capability to restore all your settings to the original default settings is always an option and can be done from here.

The first setting to adjust is the default Search Engine. Press "Search Engine" and choose between Bing, Google or Yahoo as the tool primarily used to pull results for your future searches.

Under Search Engines, you will see the section for enabling or un-enabling your device's pop-up blocker. Your device will currently be set to ask you if you want a pop-up blocked as these situations arise. You can adjust this to always block pop-ups or never block pop-ups.

Next, you will see the settings: "Accelerate Page Loading", "Optional Encryption", and "Enable Instant Page Loads". These can enable or un-unable each of these. It is recommended that you leave them at the default settings for optimal performance.

The settings section also gives you the ability to clear your web history and cookies, enable/un-enable cookies, and to give your device permission to remember the passwords you enter at various sites, and automatically populate these fields when required. The same feature can be used to remember "form data" like name/address/phone number that you may need to enter manually quite often. At any time, you can elect to remove passwords from the device's memory.

You can set your device to recognize your physical location and send you content that relates to it, such as news, events, weather, promotions, etc.

"Individual Website Data" provides information about the websites in your browsing history.

Silk can be set to ask your permission before downloading something. You should enable this, as having Silk download automatically may expose you to security threats.

The "Advanced" settings that can be enabled/un-abled are: JavaScript, security warnings, and streaming viewer. You are also able to stop your browser from loading images in this section.

Camera

The Kindle Fire HDX 7-inch comes equipped with a front-facing camera.

Taking Pictures with the Camera

Opening the camera can be done from the Home screen by swiping upward. This will take you to Grid View. Press "Camera" and you will go into camera view. There will be a circular button along the bottom of the screen. Press it once your picture is ready to be snapped.

Press the button at the bottom right to see the photo you have just taken. You can swipe through previously taken photos from this view as well.

Shooting Video with the Camera

When the camera is opened, press the button on the top left to move it to the video function. Press the red button along the bottom of the screen to begin to record. Press it a second time to stop. Press the button on the lower right of your screen to see the video you have just shot.

Note that your device stores videos it has taken itself in the Photo Library, not the Video Library.

Browsing Photos You Have Taken with the Camera

While in camera mode, press the button at the lower right of the display. It should be a screenshot of the most recently taken picture. This will pull up all your photos which you can scroll through one at a time or view in grid display.

If you would like to go back to the live camera view, press on any point in the photo to prompt a toolbar. On the right side of the bar there will be three buttons. Press the one on the left.

Productivity

Setting Up Your Email

In order to gain access to your email with the Email app, start at the Home screen. Press "Apps" and then "Email." Use the electronic keyboard to type in your email address. Gmail users will automatically be redirected to a Google site.

After you have entered the appropriate account information, you will be set up and can access your email from your device by tapping "Go to Your Inbox."

Keep in mind, your device can only sync with Gmail, Hotmail, Yahoo Mail, and AOL. POP and IMAP email systems will also work.

Using Email

When you pull up the Email App, your main email page will appear, with the Inbox front and center. From here you can read messages sent to you, compose new messages, manage folders and more.

Sending an Email

You can create and send a new email by pressing the "New" button on the top right. A blank email will come up. Type in the recipient(s), subject and body of the message here. In the top right of the screen there is a button with three dots lined up vertically. Press the button to prompt the menu for attaching photos and files, formatting, saving drafts and discarding drafts.

The "Show Formatting" feature will allow you to modify text size and style, colors, etc.

Viewing Email Folders

Press the icon on the top left with the three horizontal lines on top of each other to access your email folders. Select "Show labels" to see a list of all your folders, from which you can jump to any of them by tapping on them. Hit the back button down below to return to the main email view (the Inbox view).

Email Settings

Press the icon on the top left with the three horizontal lines on top of each other, then "Settings," and then "Email General Settings." From this view you are able to change the default message text size, show/don't show embedded images, automatically download attachments, include original messages in replies, conversations and auto-advance.

Gmail Settings

Your device is capable of adjusting your Gmail settings. While in the main email view, press the button with three horizontal lines on top of each other and then hit Settings. Further down in the Settings menu will be the "Gmail" option. With this function, you are able to sync email accounts (including their calendars and contacts), choose the inbox check frequency, as well as make a personalized email signature.

Contacts

The contacts you have in your email account(s) will also appear in your device's email feature. As you are typing in a contact for message delivery, the system will show you potential matching contacts for you to tap on to save time.

You can view/edit the contact list from the Home page by going to the Calendar or Email app.

Underneath either of these two icons there will be three options. Tap on the star and you will go to the "VIP list." Press the icon in the top right with three horizontal lines on top of each other and then press "All Contacts" if you would like to see the full listing.

Contact Settings

While in the contact folder, press the icon in the top right with three horizontal lines on top of each other, then "Settings" and then "Contacts General Settings." You now have the option to backup your Amazon contacts to the cloud (or remove the ones you have already backed up to the cloud), and also shift the order of your contacts and how you would like them to appear in your folders.

Adding a Contact

There is an easy manual way to add contacts that were not automatically synced. While in an email that came from this contact, tap down and hold on the picture or icon for them (typically alongside their email address). You will get the option to "Add to Contacts." A page containing their contact info will come up. Additional information like addresses and phone numbers can also be provided before you save the profile.

VIP's

Anyone you communicate with often or for any reason want to keep tabs of emails to/from can be saved as a "VIP." After adding someone as a new contact (paragraph above) or while editing the contact info, you can press the yellow VIP star to classify them as such.

From the main email view, press "VIP" to narrow the view to just these contacts. Keep in mind, it will not show their emails in the VIP view from before you added them.

Calendar

Accessing the calendar can be done from the Home screen by pressing "Apps" in the Navigation Bar. Press "Calendar" and it will come up. Calendar items you have in Gmail will also show up on your device's calendar for you convenience.

Changing Calendar View

Your Calendar comes set to Weekly view. You can look ahead to the upcoming week by swiping from the right of the screen to the left, and you can view the previous week(s) by reversing the motion.

On the top right is the "Today" button. Press this to view your schedule for that day in detail. Press the "Calendar" button on the top left to switch out of Week view and into Day, Month or List view.

The "List" view displays all of the appointments you have scheduled, past and future, in chronological order.

Adding Events

Press the icon with three dots on top of each other for appointment/event adding. Press "New Event" and give the event a name, location and time. You will be able to set the event to repeat and can set reminders for it. Add contacts to the event from here as well and then press "Save."

Calendar Settings

Press the button on the top left of the screen with the three parallel lines and then press "Settings" and "Calendar General Settings."

Your four options are:

-Use Default Time Zone
-Set Reminder Time
-Week Starts On
-Set Default Time Zone".

Battery Life Best Practices

Displaying Exact Percentage of Battery Remaining

The standard indicator for how much battery life your device has is a bar on your status bar which gives you a rough visual estimate. If you would like to have the precise percentage shown, slide downward to pull up the Quick Settings page.

Press Settings and then Device. From here you can enable the Show Battery Percentage feature. Once on, the number will show up on the status bar.

Conserving Battery

This device's battery should last for 11 hours if fully charged. Different types of usage consume different amounts of power, and this number could go up to 17 if you are only using it for low power purposes such as reading.

Here are some steps to make your battery life most efficient:

Notifications
You can turn all notifications off by turning "Quiet Time" on. Press the Quiet Time button in Quick Settings to do this.

Or, the notifications for individual apps and utilities can be shut off when you tap them and press Off in the menu that comes up.

Brightness
From the Quick Settings menu, press on the Brightness button and lower it.

Wireless
Turn the Airplane Mode on when you don't need wireless. From Quick Settings, press the wi-fi icon and then the Airplane Mode button.

Headphones
Use headphones instead of speakers. They can be plugged in right alongside the Volume controls.

Sleep Mode
Set your device to enter Sleep Mode sooner by pulling up the Quick Settings screen. Press "Settings" and then "Display & Sounds." Select "Display Sleep" and adjust it lower.

Email
The number of times per hour/day your device syncs with your email inbox can lowered. From the Quick Settings page, press Settings and then Applications. In Applications you need to select email, contacts, and then press the calendar button. Choose an email account and check "inbox frequency."

Security

Your device comes with numerous security features that can be adjusted based on your needs:

1-Click Purchases

This benefit is a critical security piece for your HDX. It ensures that your credit card information does not go out with each individual purchase you make. This will greatly reduce its exposure.

Wi-Fi Security

As you setup your wireless network this security setting will come up. Your device will automatically identify the type of security your wireless network is using and match it appropriately.

MAC Filtering

Certain networks screen devices based on their MAC address. If your network does, it might be necessary to add your HDX's MAC address to its router settings. This address can be found by sliding downward on the Home screen to access the Quick Settings menu. Press Wireless and the MAC address will be displayed.

Password Protecting Your Device

To better protect the information on your device should an unauthorized person get their hands on it, it is recommended that you set it to automatically lock, with a password required to unlock it prior to usage. Passwords can be added by swiping downward from the top to access Quick Settings. Press "Settings" and then "Security." The option for "Lock

Screen Password" will come up. Turn this feature on and create your 4-digit PIN.

Location-Based Services Security

Websites and apps outside of Amazon can be allowed to receive information on your location in order to send relevant information such as mapping services or local news and commercial offerings. This is controlled by Location-Based Services.

You can shut this feature off in order to tighten security. While on the Home screen, slide downward to pull up Quick Settings. Press "Settings" then "Wireless." Press the button alongside "Location-Based Services" to set it to On/Off.

Advanced Features

MayDay

Mayday is the latest tool from Amazon to help users with navigation on their devices. The goal is to make the Amazon marketplace shopping experience on your HDX as seamless as possible.

While on the Quick Settings screen, press the Mayday icon. You will be redirected to the Amazon Assist view which has the Mayday feature.

Your device does not come with Mayday automatically running. You will need to turn it on by pressing the yellow connect button. This will connect you to an Amazon technical consultant in less than 15 seconds. You will be able to see the consultant on your screen but they cannot see you. They can, however, start a remote session on your screen if you permit them to. This will let them see your screen and even perform tasks on it in order to leverage their expertise to resolve problems or work on complex settings.

You can contact Mayday for help at any time of the day, every day of the year at no cost. Currently, Mayday only has English-speaking agents.

4G Technology

Your device supports 4G LTE technology, making it capable of operating from wherever you can get a wireless signal. AT&T and Verizon both offers plans for the HDX

Links to Data Plan Offerings:

Verizon:
http://www.verizonwireless.com/wcms/consumer/shop/share-everything.html

ATT: http://www.att.com/shop/wireless/plans-new.html#fbid=7K2ASUJ66FA

Connect to 4G:
http://www.amazon.com/gp/help/customer/display.html?nodeId=201239840

http://www.amazon.com/gp/help/customer/display.html/ref=help_search_1-1?ie=UTF8&nodeId=201176350&qid=1382670989&sr=1-1

Kindle FreeTime Unlimited

As discussed earlier, you may wish to subscribe (it's a paid subscription) to FreeTime Unlimited to get instant access to children friendly content which is constantly refreshed to keep children entertained.

Amazon now offers special packages for this service to include unlimited usage for up to six children at a discounted rate. You can view the details here:

http://www.amazon.com/gp/feature.html?docId=1000863021

Subscribe to Kindle FreeTime

The FreeTime app can be accessed by pressing its icon on the Home screen. You can also go to Settings and then Parental Controls, and then press the Kindle FreeTime app icon.

Second Screen

Amazon's latest feature allows you to view video or play video games from your Amazon library on these secondary devices: Playstation 3, Playstation 4, and the 2013 Samsung Smart TV.

You gaming experience may be enhanced by using Playstation, and you can also enjoy the larger screen size on the Smart TV. Meanwhile, you can continue performing others tasks on your HDX. The HDX will also function as a remote control for the Second Screen device.

Renting Textbooks

HDX users can rent textbooks through Amazon, where they can cost as little as 20% of the list price. Rental periods normally range from 1 month to 1 year.

It is recommended that you find these textbooks on your Mac or PC, not your HDX. Visit Amazon's website and go to "Shop by Department." A menu will come up which includes "Books and Audio." Under "Books" you will find "Textbooks." Click this and you will enter the Kindle Textbooks store.

Toward the left is "Textbook Programs" in orange. Beneath it is "Textbook Rental" and then "Get Started—Rent Your Textbooks Here." Type the title(s) into the search bar to locate them.

Books available for rent (not all are) will have a toggle dot with "Rent" to the right of it. Click the dot and check out with your book. A print version will be sent out, or the eBook will be added to your electronic library, depending on what you have selected.

Immersion Reading

This is an excellent educational tool for those who are novice readers or just new to reading English.

As the audiobook is playing, the eBook will be pulled up and a highlighter will move through the text word for word at the same pace.

You can open the Immersion Reading feature through the Content Library Menu. Press "Shop" and then "Books." Hit the button on the top left with three lines and the Navigation Panel will come up. Select "Immersion Reading" and you will be able to view all content available for this feature.